SPOT THE SNOT!

15 snots,
blown far and wide.
Where could they be, I
wonder where they'll hide?

WHERE'S MR BOGEY?

WHERE'S YUCKY?

WHERE'S DRIPPY DOO?

WHERE'S GOOEY LOUIE?

WHERE'S SNOTTER?

WHERE'S SLIMY?

WHERE'S SNEEZY?

WHERE'S BOBBY BOOGER?

WHERE'S NOSEY PARKER?

WHERE'S SNOZZLE?

WHERE'S PICK AND FLICK?

WHERE'S SNOTTY?

WHERE'S LADY SNOTTINGTON?

WHERE'S GLOOPY?

GUESS WHAT?
YOU FOUND ALL THE SNOT!

The snots are leaving,
they're waving at you.
You'll see them again when
you've got the flu!

A Bonus Search

SPOT THE POO!

The two below are hiding in the book. Don't believe me? Go take a look!

THE END!

Find us on Amazon!

Discover all of the titles available in our store; including these below...

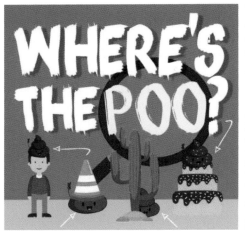

Printed in Great Britain
by Amazon